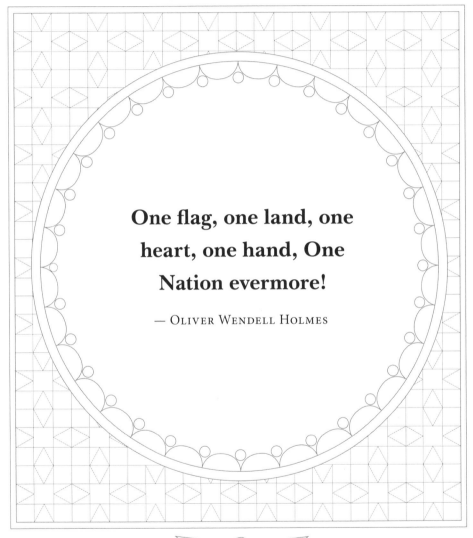

One flag, one land, one
heart, one hand, One
Nation evermore!

— OLIVER WENDELL HOLMES

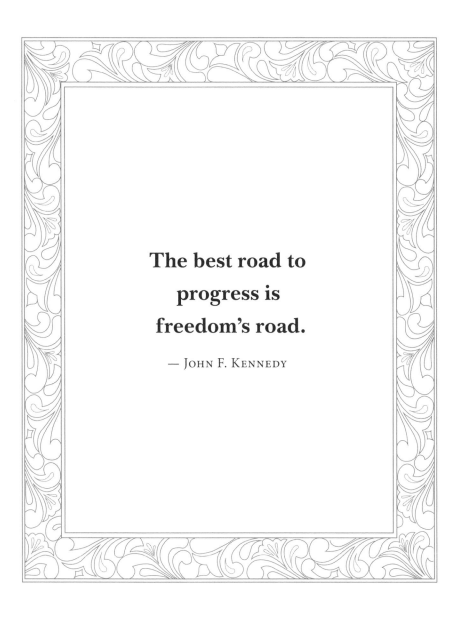

The best road to
progress is
freedom's road.

— JOHN F. KENNEDY

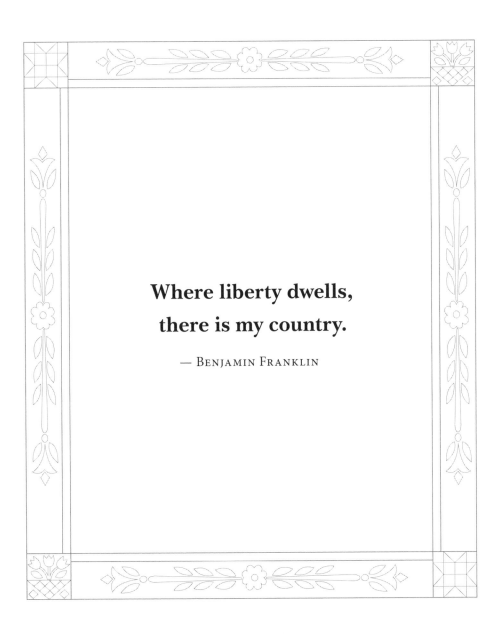

**Where liberty dwells,
there is my country.**

— Benjamin Franklin

America is another name
for opportunity.

— Ralph Waldo Emerson

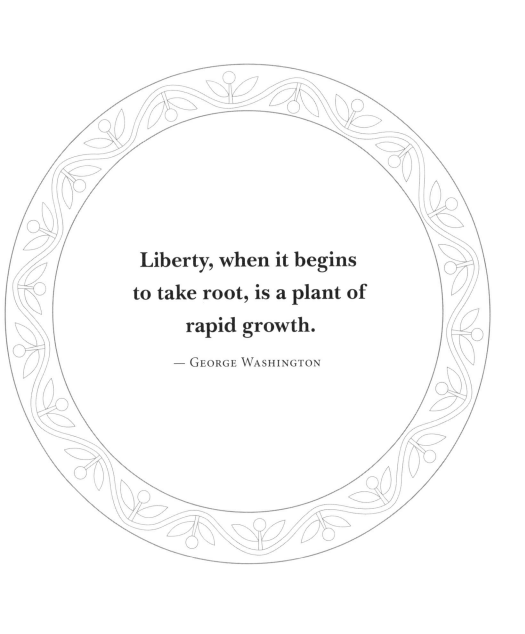

Liberty, when it begins to take root, is a plant of rapid growth.

— George Washington

All good things are wild and free.

— HENRY DAVID THOREAU

The clash of ideas is the sound of freedom.

— LADY BIRD JOHNSON

Patriotism is a thing of
the heart. A man is a
patriot if his heart beats
true to his country.

— CHARLES EDWARD JEFFERSON

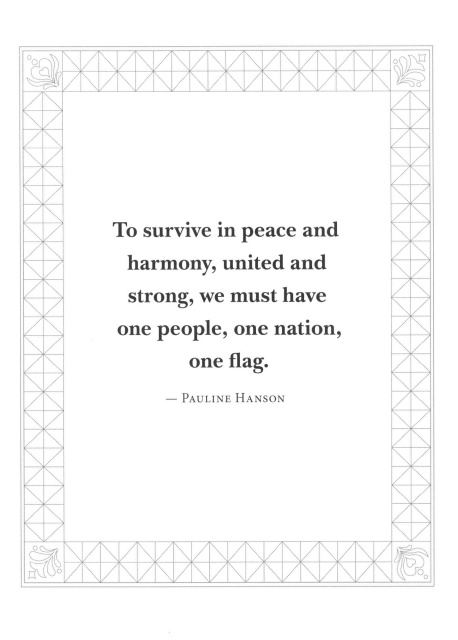

To survive in peace and harmony, united and strong, we must have one people, one nation, one flag.

— PAULINE HANSON

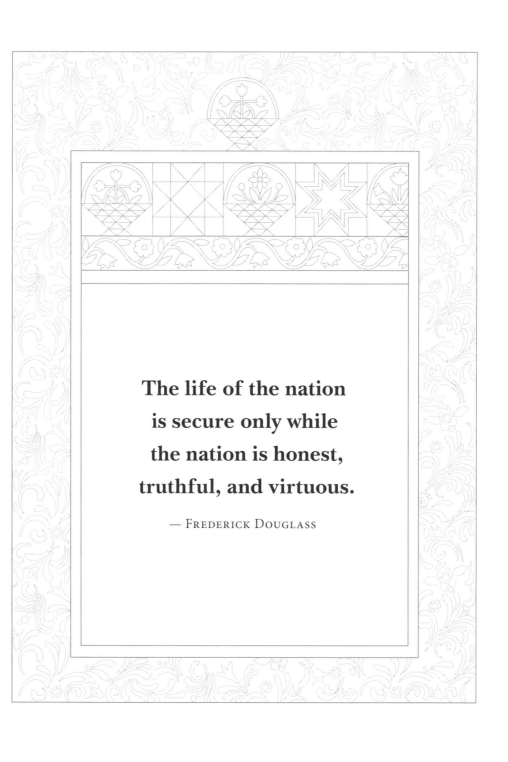

**The life of the nation
is secure only while
the nation is honest,
truthful, and virtuous.**

— Frederick Douglass

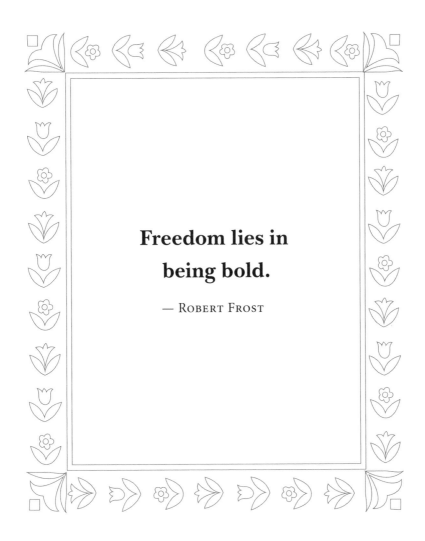

Freedom lies in being bold.

— Robert Frost

Patriotism consists not in waving the flag, but in striving that our country shall be righteous as well as strong.

— James Bryce

About Jim Shore

Jim Shore grew up in rural South Carolina, the son of artistic parents who instilled a love of American folk art. His grandmother was a master quilter who taught him the patience and skill to bring intricate designs to life. Jim worked for decades developing his craft, manufacturing his own designs, and traveling the country to sell his work. Finally, in 2001, he partnered with Enesco to create Heartwood Creek, the successful brand that brought Jim worldwide fame. Jim has received multiple awards from prestigious trade organizations, including the ICON HONORS Life Accomplishment Award in 2012. Through his partnership with Enesco, the Jim Shore Collection has grown from a small group of Santas, snowmen, and angels to a broad year-round brand respected and sold around the world. Jim's boundless creativity and unique ability enable him to touch people in all walks of life through his art.

ISBN 978-1-64178-115-2

Fox Chapel Publishing makes every effort to use environmentally friendly paper for printing.

© 2021 by Jim Shore and Quiet Fox Designs, *www.QuietFoxDesigns.com*, an imprint of Fox Chapel Publishing Company, Inc., 903 Square Street, Mount Joy, PA 17552.

We are always looking for talented authors and artists. To submit an idea, please send a brief inquiry to acquisitions@foxchapelpublishing.com.

Printed in Singapore
First printing